Handy West Virginia Genealogy Guide

Gary L. Morris

©2015 Gary L. Morris

ISBN-13: 978-1507690635

ISBN-10: 1507690630

Table of Contents

Notes

Genealogical Research in West Virginia

As one of the longest inhabited areas in America, there is a wealth of genealogical records and resources available for tracing your family history in West Virginia. Because of the abundance of information held at many different locations, tracking down the records for your ancestor can be an ominous task. Don't worry though, we know just where they are, and we'll show you which records you'll need, while helping you to understand:

1. What they are
2. Where to find them
3. How to use them

These records can be found both online and off, so we'll introduce you to online websites, indexes and databases, as well as brick-and-mortar repositories and other institutions that will help with your research in West Virginia. So that you will have a more comprehensive understanding of these records, we have provided a brief history of the "Mountain State" to illustrate what type of records may have been generated during specific time periods. That information will assist you in pinpointing times and locations on which to focus the search for your West Virginia ancestors and their records.

A Brief History of West Virginia

When the first Europeans arrived during the 1640s, older inhabitants had been driven out by the Cherokee and Iroquois, and only a few Delaware, Shawnee and Tuscarora, Indian villages remained. The area was still very active as a hunting and warring ground however, and attempts by Europeans to claim land were violently opposed.

Exploration was stimulated by the fur trade, and England claimed the Ohio Valley area, a claim opposed by France, but brought to an end by the French and Indian War. The first settlers arrived in the Berkeley County area around 1735, and by 1750 there were several thousand people settled in the eastern panhandle. Treaties were signed with the Cherokee and Iroquois, and in 1769 settlement spread into the Monongahela, Greenbrier, and upper Ohio valleys.

Settlement expanded in to other areas right up until the time of the Revolutionary War, and West Virginia was actually part of Virginia when that state entered the Union in 1788. After the War of 1812 serious differences developed between the western and eastern parts of Virginia, the majority of the eastern part being aristocratic slave-owners, the west populated by small industries and farming.

Because the easterners dominated the Virginia Legislature due to property qualifications, westerners suffered inadequate representation, poor transportation, inequitable taxes, inadequate schools, economic retardation, and undemocratic county governments. The westerners were left embittered when a constitutional convention in 1829-1830 brought no changes, and a further convention in 1850-1851, although meeting the political demands of the west, left them even more economically alienated.

When Virginia seceded from the Union in 1861, western counties loyal to the Union established the Reorganized Government and agreed to the separation of present-day West Virginia from Virginia. Congress and President Lincoln approved the move, and West Virginia became the Union's 35th State on June 20, 1863.

After the Civil War government sought to foster immigration, improve transportation, and to design a tax structure that would be attractive to businesses. Industry thrived, and much money was made from oil, coal, railroads, and timber.

Important Genealogical Dates in West Virginia History

1735 – First settlers arrive in Berkeley County area

1738 – Frederick and Augusta counties created

1782 – Battle of Fort Henry

1859 – John Brown seizes Harper's Ferry arsenal

1861 – Battle of Phillipi

1863 – Secedes from Virginia and gains Statehood

Famous Battles Fought in West Virginia

West Virginia was the site of many Civil War Battles. The battle accounts that exist can be very effective in uncovering the military records of your ancestor. They can tell you what regiments fought in which battles, and often include the names and ranks of many officers and enlisted men.

Some of the most important battles fought in West Virginia include the battles of:

Camp Alleghany
Carnifex Ferry
Cheat Mountain
Droop Mountain
Greenbrier River
Harpers Ferry
Hoke's Run
Kessler's Cross Lanes
Moorefield
Philippi
Princeton Courthouse
Rich Mountain
Shepherdstown
Smithfield Crossing
Summit Point

Accounts of these battles can be found at the website of the **Civil War Sites Advisory Commission**

Civil War Sites Advisory Commission:
http://www.nps.gov/hps/abpp/battles/bystate.htm#wv

Common West Virginia Genealogical Issues and Resources to Overcome Them

Boundary Changes: Boundary changes are a common obstacle when researching West Virginia ancestors. You could be searching for an ancestor's record in one county when in fact it is stored in a different one due to historical county boundary changes.

The **Atlas of Historical County Boundaries** can help you to overcome that problem. It provides a chronological listing of every boundary change that has occurred in the history of West Virginia.

Atlas of Historical County Boundaries:
http://publications.newberry.org/ahcbp/documents/WV_Consolidate d_Chronology.htm#Consolidated_Chronology

Name Changes: Surname changes, variations, and misspellings can complicate genealogical research. It is important to check all spelling variations. Soundex, a program that indexes names by sound, is a useful first step, but you can't rely on it completely as some name variations result in different Soundex codes. The surnames could be different, but the first name may be different too. You can also find records filed under initials, middle names, and nicknames as well, so you will need to **get creative with surname variations** and spellings in order to cover all the possibilities. For help with surname variations read our instructional article on **How to Use Soundex**.

get creative with surname variations:
http://obituarieshelp.org/blog/?p=634

How to Use Soundex: http://obituarieshelp.org/blog/?p=505

West Virginia Genealogical Organizations and Archives

Genealogical resources include not only records, but the organizations that house them, or can direct you to them. These institutions include: *Archives, Libraries, Genealogical Societies, Family History Centers, Universities, Churches, and Museums.*

Following are links to their websites, their physical addresses, and a summary of the records you can find there.

Archives and Libraries

West Virginia Division of Culture and History – County court records; manuscripts; naturalization records; historical maps, newspapers, periodicals, and photographs; county vital records; probate records, wills and deeds; Genealogy Surname Exchange

The Cultural Center
Capitol Complex
1900 Kanawha Boulevard East
Charleston, WV 25305-0300
Telephone: 304-558-0220
Fax: 304-558-2779

West Virginia Division of Culture and History:
http://www.wvculture.org/history/wvsamenu.html

Library of Virginia – Manuscript collection, tax records, military records, land records, vital records, county records, private papers, bible records and genealogies, prison records, historical maps, African American and Native American resources

800 East Broad Street
Richmond, VA 23219-8000
Telephone: 804-692-3888
Fax: 804-692-3556

Library of Virginia: http://www.lva.virginia.gov/

West Virginia Collection - Census Records, Manuscripts, Maps, Atlases, and Gazetteers, Oral Histories, Printed Ephemera Collection, Census Records, Naturalization Records, Early Virginia Court Records, West Virginia Court Records, Rare Books, Historical Newspapers, Church Records, Bible Records, Tax Lists, Land Records, Military Records, Vital Records, Wills and Deeds

West Virginia University Library
P.O. Box 6069
Morgantown, WV 26506-6069
Telephone: 304-293-3536
Fax: 304-293-3981

West Virginia Collection:
http://wvrhc.lib.wvu.edu/research/collections/

Genealogical and Historical Societies

Genealogical and historical societies have access to extensive catalogues of genealogical data. They are also able to offer expert guidance for genealogical researchers. Many members are professional genealogists who are most willing to share their expertise in finding ancestors.

West Virginia Genealogical Society – Vital records, Cemetery records, Census records, Family histories, large genealogical library which is open to the public

P.O. Box 249
Elkview, WV 25071
Telephone: 304-965-1179

West Virginia Genealogical Societyo:
http://www.rootsweb.ancestry.com/~wvgs/

The Allegheny Regional Family History Society Census records, Cemetery records, and many other genealogical resources

Post Office Box 1804
Elkins, West Virginia 26241
Email: arhfs@yahoo.com

The Allegheny Regional Family History Society:
http://pages.swcp.com/~dhickman/arfhs.html

West Virginia Mailing Lists

Mailing lists are internet based facilities that use email to distribute a single message to all who subscribe to it. When information on a particular surname, new records, or any other important genealogy information related to the mailing list topic becomes available, the subscribers are alerted to it. Joining a mailing list is an excellent way to stay up to date on West Virginia genealogy research topics. Rootsweb have an extensive listing of **West Virginia Mailing Lists** on a variety of topics.

West Virginia Mailing Lists:
http://lists.rootsweb.ancestry.com/index/usa/WV/misc.html

West Virginia Message Boards

A message board is another internet based facility where people can post questions about a specific genealogy topic and have it answered by other genealogists. If you have questions about a surname, record type, or research topic, you can post your question and other researchers and genealogists will help you with the answer. Be sure to check back regularly, as the answers are not emailed to you. The West Virginia message boards at **Rootsweb** are completely free to use.

Rootsweb:
http://boards.rootsweb.com/localities.northam.usa.states/mb.ashx

West Virginia Newspapers and Periodicals

Many genealogy periodicals and historical newspapers contain reprinted copies of family genealogies, transcripts of family Bible records, information about local records and archives, census indexes, church records, queries, land records, obituaries, court records, cemetery records, and wills. The following sites have historical West Virginia newspapers and periodicals that you can search online or on-site.

West Virginia Division of Culture and History – Large collection of newspapers from every county in the state of West Virginia dating from early 19th century to present

The Cultural Center
Capitol Complex
1900 Kanawha Boulevard East
Charleston, WV 25305-0300
Telephone: 304-558-0220
Fax: 304-558-2779

West Virginia Division of Culture and History:
http://www.wvculture.org/history/wvsamenu.html

West Virginia Collection - Approximately 1200 West Virginia Newspaper dating from1790-1990

West Virginia University Library
P.O. Box 6069
Morgantown, WV 26506-6069
Telephone: 304-293-3536
Fax: 304-293-3981

West Virginia Collection:
http://wvrhc.lib.wvu.edu/research/collections/

GenealogyBank.com – free searchable database of West Virginia newspaper archives, 1808-1904

GenealogyBank.com: http://www.genealogybank.com/gbnk/newspapers/explore/USA/West_Virginia/

The Online Books Page – links to historical West Virginia books and periodicals available for viewing online

The Online Books Page: http://onlinebooks.library.upenn.edu/webbin/book/browse?type=subject&type=subject&key=west+virginia

Library of Congress Digital Newspaper Directory – free searchable database of historical U.S. newspapers dating from 1690-present

Library of Congress Digital Newspaper Directory: http://chroniclingamerica.loc.gov/search/titles/

NewspaperArchive.com – largest online database of historical newspapers in the world.

NewspaperArchive.com: http://newspaperarchive.com/

Historical West Virginia Maps and Gazetteers

Maps are an integral part of genealogical research. They help us to
locate landmarks, towns, cities, parishes, states, provinces,
waterways and roads and streets. They also help us to determine
when and where boundary changes might have taken place, and give
us a visualization of the area we're researching in.

For locating place names, a gazetteer is the best possible resource for
any genealogist. Gazetteers are also sometimes called "place name
dictionaries", and can help you to locate the area in which you need
to conduct research. Below are links to the maps and gazetteers for
research in West Virginia.

Peabody GNIS Service – West Virginia;
http://peabody.research.yale.edu/cgi-
bin/Query.GNIS?ST=West%20Virginia&SU=1

Color Landform Atlas – West Virginia:
http://fermi.jhuapl.edu/states/wv_0.html

1985 U.S. Atlas: http://www.livgenmi.com/1895/WV/

West Virginia Hometown Locator:
http://westvirginia.hometownlocator.com/

West Virginia Collection - Statewide, regional, and county atlases,
local histories including detailed maps

West Virginia University Library
P.O. Box 6069
Morgantown, WV 26506-6069
Telephone: 304-293-3536
Fax: 304-293-3981

West Virginia Collection:
http://wvrhc.lib.wvu.edu/research/collections/

<u>West Virginia City Directories</u>
.

City directories are similar to telephone directories in that they list the residents of a particular area. The difference though is what is important to genealogists, and that is they pre-date telephone directories. You can find an ancestor's information such as their street address, place of employment, occupation, or the name of their spouse. A one-stop-shop for finding city directories in West Virginia is the **West Virginia Online Historical Directories** which contains a listing of every available online historical directory related to West Virginia. Another useful site is **US City Directories** which identifies printed, microfilmed, and online West Virginia directories and their repositories.

West Virginia Online Historical Directories:
https://sites.google.com/site/onlinedirectorysite/Home/usa/wv

US City Directories: http://www.uscitydirectories.com/sd.htm

West Virginia Genealogical Records

Birth, Death, Marriage and Divorce Records – Also known as vital records, birth, death, and marriage certificates are the most basic, yet most important records attached to your ancestor. The reason for their importance is that they not only place your ancestor in a specific place at a definite time, but potentially connect the individual to other relatives. Below is a list of repositories and websites where you can find West Virginia vital records.

West Virginia Health Statistics Center -
West Virginia Occurrence Birth Records from 1917 to Present, West Virginia Occurrence Delayed File Birth Records starting around 1850, West Virginia Occurrence Death Records from 1917 to Present, West Virginia Occurrence Marriage Indexes from 1924 to Present, West Virginia Occurrence Marriage Records from 1964 to Present, West Virginia Occurrence Divorce Indexes from 1967 to Present

350 Capital St., Room 165
Charleston, WV 25301-3701
Tel: 304-558-2931

West Virginia Health Statistics Center:
http://www.wvdhhr.org/bph/hsc/vital/genealogy.asp

West Virginia Division of Culture and History – County births, delayed births, deaths, and marriages, 1845 to late 20th century

The Cultural Center
Capitol Complex
1900 Kanawha Boulevard East
Charleston, WV 25305-0300
Telephone: 304-558-0220
Fax: 304-558-2779

West Virginia Division of Culture and History:
http://www.wvculture.org/history/wvsamenu.html

Library of Virginia – Births (1853–1896), deaths (1853–1896, 1912–1939), and marriages (1853–1935)

800 East Broad Street
Richmond, VA 23219-8000
Telephone: 804-692-3888
Fax: 804-692-3556

Library of Virginia: http://www.lva.virginia.gov/

West Virginia Genealogical Society – County births, deaths, and marriages dating from late 18th century to mid-20th century

P.O. Box 249
Elkview, WV 25071
Telephone: 304-965-1179

West Virginia Genealogical Society:
http://www.rootsweb.ancestry.com/~wvgs/

Family Search has the following indexes that can be searched online for free:

West Virginia Births and Christenings 1853-1928:
https://familysearch.org/search/collection/1708695

West Virginia Births, 1853-1930:
https://familysearch.org/search/collection/1417341

West Virginia Deaths and Burials 1854-1932:
https://familysearch.org/search/collection/1708700

West Virginia Deaths, 1804-1999:
https://familysearch.org/search/collection/1417434

West Virginia Marriages, 1780-1970:
https://familysearch.org/search/collection/1408729

West Virginia Marriages, 1854-1932:
https://familysearch.org/search/collection/1708701

Census Records

Census records are among the most important genealogical documents for placing your ancestor in a particular place at a specific time. Like BDM records, they can also lead you to other ancestors, particularly those who were living under the authority of the head of household.

Library of Virginia – Federal census records for West Virginia, 1810 through 1880, and for 1900 through 1940

800 East Broad Street
Richmond, VA 23219-8000
Telephone: 804-692-3888
Fax: 804-692-3556

Library of Virginia: http://www.lva.virginia.gov/

West Virginia Collection - Federal census records for West Virginia, 1810 through 1880, and for 1900 through 1940

West Virginia University Library
P.O. Box 6069
Morgantown, WV 26506-6069
Telephone: 304-293-3536
Fax: 304-293-3981

West Virginia Collection:
http://wvrhc.lib.wvu.edu/research/collections/

West Virginia Genealogical Society – County census records 1850-1930

P.O. Box 249
Elkview, WV 25071
Telephone: 304-965-1179

West Virginia Genealogical Society:
http://www.rootsweb.ancestry.com/~wvgs/

The **Free Census Project** has transcribed many West Virginia indexes and new material is added daily

Free Census Project: http://usgwcensus.org/cenfiles/wv.htm

Access Genealogy – West Virginia county census records dating from 1810-1930

Access Genealogy: http://www.accessgenealogy.com/census/west-virginia-census-records.htm

African American Census Schedules Online – slave schedules, mortality schedules, slave-owners census

African American Census Schedules Online: http://www.afrigeneas.com/aacensus/ga/

Native Americans in Census Records (US National Archives)

Native Americans in Census Records: http://www.archives.gov/research/census/native-americans/

West Virginia Church Records

Church and synagogue records are a valuable resource, especially for baptisms, marriages, and burials that took place before 1900. You will need to at least have an idea of your ancestor's religious denomination, and in most cases you will have to visit a brick and mortar establishment to view them.

Most church records are kept by the individual church, although in some denominations, records are placed in a regional archive or maintained at the diocesan level. Local Historical Societies are sometimes the repository for the state's older church records. Below are links archives that maintain church records, as well as a few databases that can be viewed online.

The **Family History Library** contains many church records from a variety of denominations on microfilm.

Family History Library:
http://familysearch.org/learn/wiki/en/Family_History_Library

Library of Virginia – Baptist, Christian (Disciples of Christ), Episcopal, Jewish, Lutheran and German Reformed, Methodist, Presbyterian, Roman Catholic, Society of Friends (Quakers), and Unitarian church records dating from colonial era, mostly administrative

800 East Broad Street
Richmond, VA 23219-8000
Telephone: 804-692-3888
Fax: 804-692-3556

Library of Virginia: http://www.lva.virginia.gov/

Central Repositories for Denominational Records

Church of Jesus Christ of Latter-day Saints (Mormons)

Early Mormon Church records for West Virginia can be found on film located at the LDS Family History Library in Salt Lake City and can be searched via the **Family History Library Catalog**

Family History Library Catalog:
https://familysearch.org/eng/Library/FHLC/frameset_fhlc.asp

The **Church History Library** has an even broader collection of historical church records than the Family History Library.

Church History Library
15 East North Temple
Salt Lake City, Utah 84150-1600
Phone: (801) 240-2272

Church History Library:
https://history.lds.org/?lang=eng#FlashPluginDetected

Baptist

West Virginia Baptist Historical Society
Route #2 Box 304
Ripley WV 25271
Telephone 304-372-3675

West Virginia Baptist Historical Society: http://wvbhs.tripod.com/

American Baptist - Samuel Colgate Historical Library
1106 South Goodman Street
Rochester, NY 14620-2532
Phone: (716) 473-1740
Fax: (716) 473-1740

American Baptist - Samuel Colgate Historical Library:
http://abhsarchives.org/

<u>Congregational</u>

Congregational Library
14 Beacon Street
Boston, MA 02108
Phone: (617) 523-0470
Fax: (617) 523-0470

Congregational Library http://www.14beacon.org/

<u>Presbyterian</u>

Presbyterian Historical Society
425 Lombard Street
Philadelphia, PA 19147
Telephone: 1-215-627-1852
Fax: 1-215-627-0509

Presbyterian Historical Society http://www.history.pcusa.org/

<u>Methodist</u>

Methodist Historical Society
West Virginia Wesleyan College
Annie M. Pfeiffer Library
59 College Avenue
Buckhannon, WV 26201
Telephone: 304-473-8013
Fax: 304-473-8888
Email: librarian@wvwc.edu

West Virginia Wesleyan College: http://www.wvwc.edu/

<u>Episcopal</u>

Episcopal Diocese of West Virginia
1608 Virginia Street East
P.O. Box 5400
Charleston, WV 25361
Ph: 304-344-3597
Fax: 304-343-3295

Episcopal Diocese of West Virginia: http://www.wvdiocese.org/

<u>Roman Catholic</u>

Diocese of Wheeling-Charleston – serves all of West Virginia
1300 Byron Street
P.O. Box 230
Wheeling, WV 26003
Telephone: 304-233-0880 or 1- 888-434-6237
Fax: 304-233-0890

Diocese of Wheeling-Charleston: http://www.dwc.org

West Virginia Military Records

More than 40 million Americans have participated in some kind of war service since America was colonized. The chance of finding your ancestor amongst those records is exceptionally high. Military records can even reveal individuals who never actually served, such as those who registered for the two World Wars but were never called to duty.

Below are a number of links to websites and archives that contain West Virginia military records.

Library of Virginia – Colonial service records, Revolutionary War records, Civil War records, War of 1812 records

800 East Broad Street
Richmond, VA 23219-8000
Telephone: 804-692-3888
Fax: 804-692-3556

Library of Virginia: http://www.lva.virginia.gov/

West Virginia Collection – West Virginia Civil War Service Records

West Virginia University Library
P.O. Box 6069
Morgantown, WV 26506-6069
Telephone: 304-293-3536
Fax: 304-293-3981

West Virginia Collection:
http://wvrhc.lib.wvu.edu/research/collections/

National Archives and Records Administration - World War I
Draft Registration Cards
Microfilm Roll List

8601 Adelphi Road
College Park, MD 20740-6001
Toll free: 1-866-272-6272

National Archives and Records Administration:
http://www.archives.gov/research/military/

US Department of Veterans Affairs Nationwide Gravesite Locator – includes information on veterans and their family members buried in veterans and military cemeteries having a government grave marker.

US Department of Veterans Affairs Nationwide Gravesite Locator: http://gravelocator.cem.va.gov/

You may also find your ancestor's military records in the following databases:

United States General Index to Pension Files, 1861-1934:
https://familysearch.org/search/collection/1919699

United States Index to Service Records, War with Spain, 1898:
https://familysearch.org/search/collection/1919583

United States Index to Indian Wars Pension Files, 1892-1926 – military pension records of soldiers who fought in the Indian Wars between 1817 and 1898

United States Index to Indian Wars Pension Files, 1892-1926:
https://familysearch.org/search/collection/1979427

United States Registers of Enlistments in the U.S. Army, 1798-1914 - index of men who enlisted in the United States Army, 1798-1914.

United States Registers of Enlistments in the U.S. Army, 1798-1914: https://familysearch.org/search/collection/1880762

United States Mexican War Pension Index, 1887-1926 - index to Mexican War pension files for service between 1846 and 1848

United States Mexican War Pension Index, 1887-1926: https://familysearch.org/search/collection/1979390

Civil War Soldiers Service Records - Service records for both Union and Confederate soldiers indexed by soldier's name, rank, and unit.

Civil War Soldier Service Records: http://go.fold3.com/civilwar_records/

West Virginia Cemetery Records

As convenient as it is to search cemetery records online, keep in mind that there are a few disadvantages over visiting a cemetery in person. They are:

- Tombstone information is not always accurately transcribed
- The arrangement of the graves in a cemetery can be crucial as family members are often buried next to each other or in the same grave. This arrangement is not always preserved in the alphabetical indexes that are found online.

With that information in mind, the following websites have databases that can be searched online for West Virginia Cemetery records.

West Virginia Tombstone Transcription Project - death and burial records

West Virginia Tombstone Transcription Project:
http://www.usgwtombstones.org/westvirg/westvirg.html

West Virginia Genealogical Society – Statewide cemetery record collection

P.O. Box 249
Elkview, WV 25071
Telephone: 304-965-1179

West Virginia Genealogical Society:
http://www.rootsweb.ancestry.com/~wvgs/

The Allegheny Regional Family History Society - Searchable Cemetery index of transcriptions from the Allegheny region

Post Office Box 1804
Elkins, West Virginia 26241
Email: arhfs@yahoo.com

The Allegheny Regional Family History Society:
http://pages.swcp.com/~dhickman/arfhs.html

African American Cemeteries Online – African American, slave, and Native American cemetery records

African American Cemeteries Online:
http://africanamericancemeteries.com/wv/

Access Genealogy – database of West Virginia cemetery record transcriptions

Access Genealogy:
http://www.accessgenealogy.com/cemetery/west-virginia-cemetery-records.htm

Find a Grave – over 100 million grave records can be searched on this site. Search can be conducted by name, location, or cemetery name.

Find a Grave: http://www.findagrave.com/

Interment.net - A free online database containing approximately 4 million cemetery records from around the world.

Interment.net: http://www.interment.net/

Billion Graves – as the name implies, you can search a billion records including headstone photos, transcriptions, cemetery records, and grave locations.

Billion Graves:
http://billiongraves.com/pages/search/index.php#cemetery

West Virginia Obituaries

Obituaries can reveal a wealth about our ancestor and other relatives. You can search our **West Virginia Obituaries Listings** from hundreds of West Virginia newspapers online for free.

West Virginia Obituaries Listings:
http://obituarieshelp.org/west_virginia_newspaper_obituaries.html

West Virginia Wills and Probate Records

The documents found in a probate packet may include a complete inventory of a person's estate, newspaper entries, witness testimony, a copy of a will, list of debtors and creditors, names of executors or trustees, names of heirs. They can not only tell you about the ancestor you're currently researching, but lead to other ancestors.

West Virginia Division of Culture and History – Wills, deeds, estate settlements, mid 19th century to late 20th century

The Cultural Center
Capitol Complex
1900 Kanawha Boulevard East
Charleston, WV 25305-0300
Telephone: 304-558-0220
Fax: 304-558-2779

West Virginia Division of Culture and History:
http://www.wvculture.org/history/wvsamenu.html

Library of Virginia – Wills and deeds from early 18th century to circa 1900's

800 East Broad Street
Richmond, VA 23219-8000
Telephone: 804-692-3888
Fax: 804-692-3556

Library of Virginia: http://www.lva.virginia.gov/

West Virginia Collection - Wills, Deeds, Probates, Estate Records, Personal Property Books, dating from mid 18th century

West Virginia University Library
P.O. Box 6069
Morgantown, WV 26506-6069
Telephone: 304-293-3536
Fax: 304-293-3981

West Virginia Collection:
http://wvrhc.lib.wvu.edu/research/collections/

Family Search has the following indexes that can be searched online for free:

West Virginia Will Books, 1756-1971:
https://familysearch.org/search/collection/1909099

West Virginia Immigration and Naturalization Records

The naturalization process generated many types of records, including petitions, declarations of intention, and oaths of allegiance. These records can provide family historians with information such as a person's birth date and place of birth, immigration year, marital status, spouse information, occupation, witnesses' names and addresses, and more.

If your ancestor lived in or near a large city, or near a city where U.S. courts convened, you may find naturalization records in the **U.S. District Court** before 1906.

U.S. District Court:
http://www.uscourts.gov/FederalCourts/UnderstandingtheFederalCourts/DistrictCourts.aspx

For the rural areas of West Virginia, naturalization records may be found with the **County Courts** in each county. Often the records were mixed in with other court proceedings making them difficult to locate. A few counties kept separate records for naturalization. After 1906, all naturalizations were handled in Federal District Courts.

County Courts:
http://www.50states.com/west_virginia/state_courts.htm

West Virginia Division of Culture and History – Naturalization Law Orders, Naturalization Petitions and Records, Declarations of Intention, Petitions and Declarations of Intention, Petitions Denied and Granted, early to mid 20th century

The Cultural Center
Capitol Complex
1900 Kanawha Boulevard East
Charleston, WV 25305-0300
Telephone: 304-558-0220
Fax: 304-558-2779

West Virginia Division of Culture and History:
http://www.wvculture.org/history/wvsamenu.html

West Virginia Collection – Naturalization Index, Declaration of Intent Books, Petitions & Records

West Virginia University Library
P.O. Box 6069
Morgantown, WV 26506-6069
Telephone: 304-293-3536
Fax: 304-293-3981

West Virginia Collection:
http://wvrhc.lib.wvu.edu/research/collections/

US National Archives – Immigration records, Naturalization records, Ship's Passenger lists

The National Archives and Records Administration
8601 Adelphi Road
College Park, MD 20740-6001
Tel: 1-866-272-6272; 1-86-NARA-NARAS

US National Archives: http://www.archives.gov/research/guide-fed-records/groups/085.html

Family Search has the following indexes which can be searched online for free:

West Virginia Naturalization Records, 1814-1991:
https://familysearch.org/search/collection/1909003

West Virginia Native American Records

Library of Virginia – Legislative petitions, Indian school files, Missionaries reports, various state records, marriage records, county court records, bible records, census records

800 East Broad Street
Richmond, VA 23219-8000
Telephone: 804-692-3888
Fax: 804-692-3556

Library of Virginia: http://www.lva.virginia.gov/

National Archives and Records Administration - Dawes Commission Final Cards of the Five Civilized Tribes

8601 Adelphi Road
College Park, MD 20740-6001
Toll free: 1-866-272-6272

National Archives and Records Administration: http://www.archives.gov/research/military/

Access Genealogy – West Virginia Native American census records, tribal histories, and much more

Access Genealogy: http://www.accessgenealogy.com/native/west-virginia-indian-tribes.htm

U.S. National Archives - information on American Indians who maintained their ties to Federally-recognized Tribes (1830-1970).

U.S. National Archives: http://www.archives.gov/research/native-americans/

Records of the Bureau of Indian Affairs (BIA)

Records of the Bureau of Indian Affairs (BIA): http://www.archives.gov/research/guide-fed-records/groups/075.html

American Indians Records Repository - records dating from the 1700s including trust, education and other historic Indian Affairs records

American Indian Records Repository
Meritex Enterprises
17501 West 98th Street
Lenexa, KS 66219
Phone: 913-888-0601

American Indians Records Repository:
http://www.doi.gov/ost/records_mgmt/american-indian-records-repository.cfm

Missing Matriarchs – Resources for Researching Female West Virginia Ancestors

Looking for female ancestors requires an adjustment of how we view traditional records sources. A woman's identity was often under that of her husband, and often individual records for them can be difficult to locate. The following resources are effective in locating female ancestors in West Virginia where traditional records may not reveal them.

Bibliographies

- *Appalachian Women: An Annotated Bibliography,* Sidney S. Farr (University of Kentucky Press, 1981)
- *Coal Miner's Wives: Portraits of Endurance,* Carol A. Giesen (University Press of Kentucky 1995)
- *Missing Chapters II: West Virginia Women in History,* Frances S. Hensley (West Virginia Women's Commission, 1986)

Selected Resources for West Virginia Women's History

Women's History Museum
Box 209
108 Walnut St.
West Liberty, WV 26074

Women's Studies Program
West Virginia University
200 Clark Hall
Morgantown, WV 26506

West Virginia Women's Commission
1900 Kanawha Blvd E
Charleston, WV 25305

Common West Virginia Surnames

The following surnames are among the most common in West Virginia and are also being currently researched by other genealogists. If you find your surname here, there is a chance that some research has already been performed on your ancestor.

Agnes, Amy, Arlinda, Artis, Austin, Avent, Bailey, Barbara, Battle, Bessie, Betty, Birchett, Blackwell, Bland, Blizzard, Boney, Brooks, Brown, Butler, Butts, Carey, Chandler, Charlotte, Cherry, Christian, Christina, Claiborne, Clark, Claudetta, Clyter, Cobb, Cogdell, Coles, Coley, Collier, Cook, Cooper, Cora, Crawley, Crockett, Crumpton, Curry, Curtis, Davenport, Delia, Dice, Dorothy, Dubby, Elnora, Elsie, Evans, Fannie, Fanny, Field, Flynn, Fox, Garrett, Gaskins, Geddie, Georgia, Giles, Gillespie, Gordon, Grant, Graves, Gray, Gwaltney, Hawkins, Hayes, Henderson, Henton, Hildred, Hughes, Hunter, Jackson, Jane, Jiles, Johnson, Jones, Joyner, Keesee, King, Kiture, Laura, Lawson, Layola, Lee, Lewis, Louisa, Lucy, Lyons, Mae, Maggie, Mariah, Marie, Mary, Mason, Matil, McCadden, McKenley, Melinda, Moore, Mormon, Moton, Nannie, Narsis, Neal, Nettie, Neverson, Palmer, Pam, Parker, Peggie, Pickard, Pope, Powell, Price, R, Ralph, Redd, Robin, Rochelle, Rosa, Ross, Russell, Sandy, Sarah, Sewell, Siddle, Slade, Smith, Sophie, Spratley, Stith, Sutton, Sydnee, Tabron, Taylor, Thornton, Threatt, Tobias, Totten, Turner, Urguhart, Walker, Wallace, Waller, Waltington, Ward, Washington, Weatherford, Wehner, Welch, Wheeler, Whiting, Wiliams, Williams, Williamson, Willie, Willis, Winfield, Winnie, Young

About the Author

Gary L. Morris worked from 2009 to 2014 as a professional researcher for a major player in the genealogy field. After tracing his family lineage back to 1683, he found that genealogy could be an expensive undertaking. As such, has decided to publish these helpful guides to share the valuable free information he has discovered during his career to help others trace their family lineages as inexpensively as possible. An avid genealogist himself, he hopes you will find this guide factual, thorough, helpful, and most of all, effective in helping you to find your family members.

Notes

Notes

www.ingramcontent.com/pod-product-compliance
Lightning Source LLC
Chambersburg PA
CBHW061802280526

45787CB00003BA/1453

9 781507 690635